# PATRICK
## DES JARLAIT

# pATRick des jARlaiT

## The sTORy of an AMERicAN iNdiAN ARTisT

### As Told To NEVA williAMS

LERNER publicATiONS COMPANY
MiNNEApolis, MiNNESOTA

*Our thanks to Mrs. Ramona Des Jarlait for providing reproductions of Mr. Des Jarlait's paintings.*

LIBRARY OF CONGRESS CATALOGING IN PUBLICATION DATA

Des Jarlait, Patrick.
    Patrick Des Jarlait: the story of an American Indian artist.

    (Voices of the American Indian)
    SUMMARY: An autobiography of an American Indian artist
concentrating on his early years growing up on the Red Lake
Indian Reservation in Minnesota and highlighting his develop-
ment as an artist.

    1. Des Jarlait, Patrick, 1921-1972—Juvenile literature. [1. Des
Jarlait, Patrick, 1921-1972. 2. Chippewa Indians—Biography.
3. Indians of North America—Biography. 4. Painters] I. Williams, Neva. II. Title. III. Series.

E99.C6D477 1975      977.6'82 00497 [B] [92]      74-33523
ISBN 0-8225-0642-4

Published simultaneously in Canada by
J. M. Dent & Sons Ltd., Don Mills, Ontario

Manufactured in the United States of America

International Standard Book Number: 0-8225-0642-4
Library of Congress Catalog Card Number: 74-33523

# CONTENTS

## ILLUSTRATIONS

# pREfACE

I first became acquainted with Patrick Des Jarlait in Minneapolis, in 1970. From our first meeting, I was intrigued by his vivid paintings and by the stories he told about his life on the Red Lake Indian Reservation.

Patrick had a way of captivating his audiences with tales of his people's way of life. His manner of telling stories reminded me of the way the old Indian storytellers told their tales. The more I listened, the more I began to feel that these stories should be preserved, as a record of the fascinating heritage of the Chippewa people.

In 1972, I began to interview Patrick and to record his story. The tape recordings that were made at these interviews formed the basis for this book about the story of his life.

Minneapolis, Minnesota
June, 1975                                            NEVA WILLIAMS

The Red Lake Indian Reservation, located in northern Minnesota, covers a total area that is about the size of the state of Rhode Island. This area includes the Upper and Lower Red lakes, which together are known to be the largest body of fresh water within any one state in the United States.

The Reservation is owned by the Red Lake Chippewa Band. The people of the Band earn their living by using the abundant natural resources at Red Lake—timber, wild game, fish, and wild rice. The Chippewa work constantly to find more efficient ways of using these resources. At the same time, they continue to preserve the natural beauty of their forests and lakes, so that all people can enjoy the splendor of this vast wilderness country.

# PART ONE

# GROWING UP AT RED LAKE

Patrick Des Jarlait (DEE zhar-LAY) was an American Indian painter who belonged to the Red Lake Chippewa Band of northern Minnesota. He became known throughout the United States for his vivid paintings of Chippewa life and for his contributions to the preservation of knowledge about Red Lake Indian customs.

Patrick's interest in art began in his early childhood. Even at the age of five, he loved to draw and sketch. But perhaps no one in the Red Lake Band could have predicted that Patrick would someday be a famous painter.

During Patrick's childhood, the people of the Red Lake Reservation still followed many of the old Chippewa traditions. They led simple lives, and their activities changed with the changing of the seasons. Patrick grew up with this simple way of life and participated in the work and the traditional pastimes of his people. And all the while, he was observing and remembering what he saw around him.

In this book, he has told the story of his life, and of the rich heritage of Chippewa culture that became the subject for his most famous paintings.

# 1 EARLY YEARS AT RED LAKE

My name is Patrick Des Jarlait. I was born on the Red Lake Indian Reservation on March 1, 1921.

My earliest memories of the Red Lake Reservation have a storybook quality. I remember beautiful tall trees, sparkling blue water, and pure white snow. There were acres of forest land on the reservation, and the clear lakes held almost every kind of Minnesota fish. Nature had provided a perfect setting for a young Indian boy growing up. I spent many hours of my childhood wandering through the woods, either by myself or with my friends. And in the forests that surrounded my home, I found the animals and woodland scenes that became the subjects for my first drawings.

I remember happy days as a small child with my parents and my six brothers and sisters. I was the middle child: two brothers and one sister were older than I, and two brothers and one sister were younger. My mother and father had their work cut out for them in providing all of us with food and security, but they seemed to enjoy our family life.

Like many men of the Red Lake Tribe, Father worked as a wood-cutter for the Red Lake Lumber Mill. The mill was in the village of Redby, a mile and a half away from our house. When I reached school age, Father became an independent lumber man and took contracts for cutting pulp wood and logs. Then he worked very long hours. On many winter nights he did not get home with his horse and sleigh until after dark.

The house that we lived in was built by my father. Most of my friends lived in small one- or two-room frame houses that were covered with tar paper. But our house was made of logs. It was warm and well built, with one very large room, which we used as both living room and kitchen, and three bedrooms. Since my older brothers and sister lived at boarding school most of the year, there was plenty of room in the house for our family.

Like most houses on the reservation, our cabin was lighted with kerosene lamps. Our heat came from two wood-burning stoves—one huge barrel stove, used only for heating, and another stove used for both cooking and heating. We also used these stoves to heat water for our baths, which we took in a large, round tub.

As a boy, one of my chores was to keep enough wood piled outside the door to burn through the cold winter nights. I remember chopping both green wood and dry wood. This combination made a fire that lasted all night. I spent many winter evenings near the warm fire sketching by the light of a kerosene lamp.

From my earliest childhood, I loved to draw and sketch. My mother was often bothered by the constant disappearance of our family's paper writing tablet. My desire to sketch my surroundings continued even during a temporary blindness that I experienced as a child. Mother told me that when I was five years old, I contracted a disease called trachoma. This ailment was common among Indian families in those days, and it often caused total blindness.

Being blind was like living in a long period of night. My brothers and sisters had to lead me around the house. But I was not frightened, and I never lost the strong desire to scribble and sketch for entertainment. I was sure that I would recover, but the doctors at Red Lake Hospital told my parents that I had little chance of regaining my sight. They did not have the medicine in those days to treat trachoma and many other contagious diseases common to the Indian people. When I finally recovered my sight completely, it was like a miracle.

# 2 WINTER ON THE RESERVATION

When I was growing up, each season of the year meant the beginning of a new round of activities for the people at Red Lake. Winter was the time of year for hunting and trapping. One of my duties was to snare rabbits for our food supply, and I remember having my own trap line when I was very young. Every day I walked from trap to trap with my companion, a big dog that looked like a collie. From the traps I collected the day's catch, which usually amounted to three or four rabbits. The rabbits that I snared were hung in a little shed near our cabin. This shed was our frozen food locker, where we kept our wild game until Mother needed it for a meal. In it we stored venison, bear, moose, ducks, geese, partridge, squirrels, racoons, and fish, as well as rabbits. Rabbit was one of my favorite foods. Mother made a delicious stew by adding vegetables, wild rice, and seasoning to the delicately flavored rabbit. It was a special treat to eat the reheated stew before going to bed.

One of our staple foods during the winter was venison. My father and brothers had little trouble finding deer tracks in the deep winter snow, and they shot many deer. But even in early childhood it hurt me to see a deer slaughtered. I often watched these graceful animals in the woods during the day, and in the evenings I would sketch them. I never shot a deer, and as I grew older, my desire not to harm any animal became even stronger. Other than rabbits, the only animal I ever hunted as a little boy was the squirrel.

In addition to hunting rabbits, deer, and other wild game, the Indians also did some winter fishing. Fishing in the winter was difficult, because the lakes were entirely frozen over. The fishermen had to chop holes in the thick ice in order to fish. A line with a bright lure and a hook at the end was lowered into the water. When a fish bit the hook, it was pulled up through the hole. Since the fish were frozen immediately after being caught, we had the finest in fresh-frozen fish.

Our winter activities were not always limited to work. One of the things I looked forward to in winter was a ride in our family sleigh. Our sleigh was very unusual because it was enclosed—it looked like a big rectangular box fastened to metal runners. Father's two strong horses pulled the sleigh through the snow. Inside were benches, a table, and a stove to keep the passengers warm. The driver sat outside at the front of the sleigh. When he got cold, another driver would take his place while he warmed himself inside. Riding in the sleigh was always a special treat for me. Mother would pack a lunch so that we could stay out all day and enjoy our ride. I have vivid memories of those rides through the forests, and of looking through the windows at the beautiful trees and clean snow as we glided along.

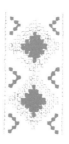

# 3  SPRING THAW

As the snow began to melt, the Indian people looked forward to one of nature's very special harvests. For it was in early spring that the sap started to flow in the maple trees, and we began to think about the rewards of sweet maple sugar and maple sugar cakes.

When signs of warmer weather appeared, the families of the reservation collected all their equipment for harvesting maple sap. Then they set up camps and built temporary birch bark shelters near the maple groves. These maple sugar camps, called "The Sugar Bush" by the older people, were a cooperative activity for the families at Red Lake. Because woodcutting occupied all my father's time, our family did not join in the maple sugar camp. But many of our relatives did, and I was always welcome to watch and to sketch them as they worked. Sketching their activities fascinated me, and the people I drew often asked to keep my pictures. They called me "the little boy with the pencil."

The first step in harvesting the maple sap was to tap the maple trees. This was done with a carved wooden peg that had a little groove down the center and one sharp, pointed end. The men tapped these pegs gently into the maple trees at a slight downward angle. From every peg they hung a birch bark basket or an old syrup can. The sap flowed along the grooved pegs and down into the containers. Every morning a man with a horse-drawn sleigh carried large washtubs from tree to tree, gathering the sap from each container. After each one had been emptied, it was hung back on the peg to catch the next day's flow of sap.

At the camps, the sap was poured into large black iron kettles that hung over a fire. Then the sap was cooked until most of the water boiled out, leaving a thick syrup. It took 30 to 40 gallons of the sweet, watery sap to make one gallon of maple syrup. Some of the syrup was poured into large troughs, where a woman stirred it gently with a flat wooden paddle. Soon the syrup was transformed into fine grains of sugar.

Some syrup was poured into small wooden molds, where it hardened into little maple cakes. After many hours of smelling the sweet aroma of cooking sap, the children could hardly wait to eat the sugar and the candy. For a special treat, we poured hot syrup on the snow and let it harden. Then we could pull it back and forth like taffy until we had a soft, chewy candy.

After about two weeks the sap in the trees began to turn bitter, and the people gathered their things together and returned home with their harvest. Many families then took sugar and syrup to Bemidji, the nearest city, where they sold it to grocery stores and tourist shops.

Selling maple sugar, however, was not a major means of livelihood at Red Lake. More important was the commercial fishing industry. The Indians caught huge quantities of fish in the spring, and many of these fish were sold and shipped to areas outside of Red Lake. The best fish in the lake were walleye pike, and the Red Lake fisheries got large contracts for catching them.

When the ice began to break up and melt in the big lakes, the Indians would begin to get their fishing nets ready. In the evenings, the men rowed their boats to the fishing grounds, often three or four miles out in the lake. There they set their nets in the deep water. The next morning, at about 5:00 A.M., the men, women, and children would gather at the docks. As a little boy, I always looked forward to the excitement of these early morning gatherings.

The men would board their hand-built boats, two men to a boat, and row out to the fishing grounds. There they found the nets and pulled up their catches of pike. There were very few other kinds of fish in the nets, because the Indian fishermen knew fish habits. They knew that each kind of fish has its own grounds and water depths, and they put their nets in just the right places to catch walleye pike. At times, the men had such a good catch that they had to make two trips.

The women and children waited anxiously on the shores for the men to return. When the boats came in, we immediately began to take the fish out of the nets and put them in boxes of crushed ice. Then trucks from the fisheries came to pick up the boxes. We often took some of the fresh fish home and cooked them. Pike was, and still is, a food that is served almost daily in Red Lake Indian homes.

Not all of the fish at Red Lake were caught by professional fishermen. As a boy, I loved to go fishing with my friends. We often packed a lunch and spent the whole day fishing in small rivers and streams. Our simple fishing poles were made of willow sticks, and we used worms and minnows to bait our hooks. We fished for bass, crappies, perch, pike, and any other fish that lived in the streams. Our fishing season began in the springtime and lasted all through the summer.

# 4   SUMMER GAMES

The summer season was a time when I got together with other children for outdoor activities and games. Some of the games we played were the same ones that girls and boys play today. Hide-and-seek, kick-the-can, and cowboys-and-Indians were our favorites. I remember that most of the boys wanted to play the part of the cowboy. For these games we often built forts or platform tree houses in the woods, constructing them out of branches and logs.

Most of the toys we played with were made by our parents or grandparents. The women made little plain-faced leather dolls for the girls. These dolls, with their beadwork trimmings, are collector's items today. Fathers made miniature wooden cradle boards for the girls and carved wooden toys for the boys. Some of the little wooden guns they made were very detailed.

In the imaginative games we played, we created a world all our own. We especially liked to play circus, complete with clowns, trained animals, and Kool-aid or lemonade, which we sold to the adults. We often included our pets in this game—our trained circus animals were dogs, cats, and sometimes tame racoons or chipmunks.

The summer event that everyone, both adults and children, looked forward to most was the Fourth of July Red Lake Pow-Wow. The traditional Pow-Wow of our forefathers had been a meeting of Indian leaders for the purpose of solving their tribal problems. But when I was a boy, the Pow-Wow was mainly a social activity. It lasted for four days, and it was the most colorful and exciting event of the year. Indian families came from other reservations and even other states to participate. White tourists were invited to come, too, and they enjoyed the activities as much as their Indian hosts did.

The Red Lake Pow-Wow could be compared to a fair. Display booths were set up in a large circle, and there the Indians sold food and craft work. During the winter the women worked on quilts, beadwork, and birchwork. These beautiful handmade items were sold at the Pow-Wow, along with Indian bread, maple sugar, and wild rice.

Dancing was one of the most colorful events at the Pow-Wow. I was always fascinated by the skill and grace of the dancers who competed for prizes. The Indians took great pride in expressing themselves through the art of dancing, and I loved to watch their twisting, turning movements as they kept time to the beat of the drums. The costumes that the dancers wore were beautifully handcrafted and very colorful. They were usually made of black velvet or felt, since black is the predominant background color in the traditional costume of the woodland Indian. Intricate floral beadwork designs in bright colors like red, yellow, and turquoise were sewn on the black background. Making these designs required hours of careful handwork, and the finished costumes were among the most beautiful expressions of Chippewa art.

Another Pow-Wow event that I enjoyed watching was the moccasin game. This game was a study of facial expression played by two teams of four players each. Each member of one team stood in front of a moccasin, under which a marble was hidden. Three of the moccasins concealed ordinary marbles, but one moccasin hid a special "steelie" marble. A player from the other team tried to guess which moccasin hid the special marble. The players on the first team had to keep a straight face— a gesture or facial expression might give away the team's secret. This game was very popular when I was young, and people often played it in their homes during the long winter months.

The greased pole contest was another challenge to everyone at the Pow-Wow. A tall pole was covered with heavy grease and placed in an upright position. Anyone could try to climb it, and whoever succeeded was given an award. It was always fun to watch the climbers' attempts, even though most were unsuccessful.

The Indian people looked forward to the Pow-Wow every year. It was a time when old friends were reunited and new friends were made. Even as an adult, I continued to enjoy taking my family back to Red Lake, where we visited family and friends and attended various celebrations. And the biggest event for us was always the Red Lake Pow-Wow.

*Chippewa Dancer*

*Maple Sugar Spring*

*Wild Rice Harvest*

*Mother and Child*

*Father and Child*

*Chippewa Preparing for Battle*

*The Red Lake Fishermen*

# 5   fAll hARVEST

As summer ended, the people began to prepare for the rice harvest, the most important event of the fall season. Wild rice was a staple food for the Indian, and it was prepared in various ways. It could be cooked and used as a cereal, parched, or combined with meat in main dishes like the rabbit stew my mother made.

The wild rice was usually ready for harvest in early September. The harvest was a family affair—adult men and women gathered and processed the rice, and the children were responsible for chores such as collecting fire wood. Families traveled from Red Lake to the White Earth Reservation, which was about 50 miles away. Red Lake was one of the few areas in that part of the country where wild rice was not plentiful. But the people at White Earth were happy to share their rice with people from Red Lake.

Wild rice is a grain, like wheat or barley. But unlike other grains, wild rice grows best in shallow, clay-bottomed lakes. Rice fields have always looked to me like wheat fields sitting in the middle of a lake.

Harvesting the wild rice was a skill in which the Indians took pride. They knew that wild rice does not ripen all at the same time. So they harvested only the rice that was ready and left the remaining kernels to ripen for a few days. It took many years of experience to learn how to harvest wild rice successfully.

Hand-built boats with boxes in the middle were used for the harvest. A man standing in the front of the boat would move it through the field with a long pole. Usually a woman sitting in the back of the boat would gather the rice. She used two tapered flails, which were cedar sticks about 18 inches long. With one flail she would bend the rice stalks over the boat. With another flail, she tapped the ripened rice gently so that it fell into the boxed area of the boat. When the boats were filled, the harvesters returned to shore, where the rice was stored in containers.

After all the rice had been harvested, it was put in large metal kettles and hung over a fire for parching. In the parching process, the rice was heated until the tough hulls that covered it burst open. Then the hulls and kernels were stirred gently. After parching, the rice was poured into a hole in the ground that was lined with buckskin. Pegs held the buckskin down on all sides. Then, a man called the "trampler" danced in the rice in order to separate the hulls from the kernels. The trampler had to wear spotlessly clean moccasins that had never touched the ground. According to an old Indian superstition, the rice harvest would be poor the following year if the trampler did not have clean moccasins.

When the trampler had finished his work, the rice was turned over to the women. They put a portion of the rice into a large, flat birch basket. Then they picked the basket up and poured the rice into another similar basket. As the rice was poured, the wind blew the hulls away from the kernels. After this "winnowing" process was repeated 30 or 40 times, the rice was clean and ready for use or storage. Wild rice prepared in the old Indian way left the long grains whole, whereas our modern commercial method often breaks the grains of rice.

After the usual two-week harvest was completed, the Red Lake families returned to their homes. Soon the rice fields and lakes would be frozen over, and the yearly cycle of activities would begin again.

# PART TWO

# A WIDER WORLD

Eventually, Patrick Des Jarlait had to leave the shelter and the traditional life of the Red Lake Reservation. During his school days, he had his first important contacts with the white people's way of life. This experience influenced him in two ways. First, it gave him a chance to explore the world and to learn many new skills. Second, it strengthened his desire to preserve and record the traditions of his own people.

Although his teachers at school did not always encourage his interest in art, Patrick kept on drawing his people and their activities. Then, with some unexpected help along the way, he started to gain the experience he would need to begin his career as an artist.

# 6 school days

My first school was St. Mary's Catholic Mission School in the village of Redby. All the Indian children had to live at the school, even though some of our homes were only half a mile away. On some weekends we had home visitation privileges. But during the week we lived in dormitories and ate all our meals at St. Mary's. Many families needed the school's help to feed their children, since jobs were hard to find, and some people were very poor. At school the children could eat the nutritious fruit, eggs, and milk that they seldom had at home. St. Mary's also provided uniforms for the children to wear.

Our lives at St. Mary's were dominated by Catholic

traditions. In the mornings we went to Mass before breakfast. My teachers were nuns and priests, and they taught us about the Church, as well as about regular academic subjects.

I remember that strict regulations regarding customs and language were placed on the Chippewa children. We were not allowed to speak to each other in Chippewa, or to participate in activities related to our heritage, like Indian games, dancing, or craft work. By imposing these restrictions, the school hoped to encourage Indian children to accept the white man's way of life.

While we were at the school, we missed our families and our homes. Sometimes my mother would let me know when she was coming to the village during the week, and I would plan to meet her on the road. She always brought me a sweet treat or fruit.

We all looked forward to the church holidays that were celebrated at St. Mary's. Christmas was especially exciting, and everyone in the community joined in the celebration at the mission. We usually spent a few days at home during the holidays, too. There was always a small tree in our living room with presents from our parents under the boughs. We enjoyed our vacation, and we never looked forward to going back to the school routine.

When I was about seven years old, my mother died. This was a period of sadness and change in our family. The older children assumed many of the chores and responsibilities of the household. In time, my father remarried, and we moved to a nice house in the village of Red Lake.

At about the time of our move, I was transferred from St. Mary's to the Red Lake Agency Boarding School. My friends and I looked forward to this change, because we knew we would have more privileges there and more time for sports and activities. At St. Mary's, our religious obligations had left us little time for play.

But in some ways, life at the Red Lake school was similar to that in the mission school. We lived in dormitories and ate all our meals at school. Every Sunday, we marched a mile and a half to the mission for church services, even though the temperatures would sometimes fall to 25 degrees below zero or colder during the winter. And there were strict regulations placed on our use of Chippewa customs and language, as there had been at St. Mary's. During the summers at home, we were not under these restrictions, and we returned to our Indian ways.

But we did have more time for going to movies and for other kinds of recreation. I also continued my interest in art. At St. Mary's, some of the nuns had encouraged my drawing and had given me religious subjects to sketch. But I remember having my ears pulled by the priests because I was sketching during study time. At Red Lake Boarding School, I was allowed to plan decorations for school affairs. Since the workshop was always available, I became interested in carving and building things out of wood. My father was a skilled carpenter and appreciated my interest in woodwork.

Although my teachers at the Red Lake Agency School allowed me to sketch during study time, I don't remember getting much encouragement from them. In those days, an art career was not practical for a reservation Indian. I thought that I would always live on the reservation and that I would eventually earn my living in the lumber mill or at the fisheries. It didn't occur to me at that time that there was any other way of life open to me. This was to change, however, when I transferred to Pipestone Boarding School in Pipestone, Minnesota.

# 7  A TURNING POINT

My experience at Pipestone Boarding School was an important turning point for me. During those years, I realized for the first time that there was something more than reservation life.

At Pipestone we had opportunities to meet white people and to learn about their way of life. We made extra money by doing yard work, painting, and other part-time jobs for white families. The families were always very friendly and sometimes invited us to have Sunday dinner with them. In addition to meeting white families, I got acquainted with my Indian classmates, who came from all over the United States. These experiences had an influence on my attitudes and my plans for the future.

There were many new activities and new things to explore at Pipestone. The world-famous Pipestone Quarry was located close to our school. This is the only deposit of pipestone in the world, as far as anyone knows. For centuries the Indians have used pipestone to carve their ceremonial peace pipes. Indian tribes from all over North America traveled to this location to get pipestone. Before it is exposed to air, this red stone is fairly soft and easy to carve into many shapes. I liked to carve souvenir items out of pipestone, and I earned extra money by selling my carvings to tourist shops.

One of my most important activities during these years was my work with the Boy Scouts. I was an active member of a Boy Scout troop for three years, and I earned badges in woodcarving and art. My most outstanding memory was a Boy Scout trip to Sioux Falls, South Dakota. There I was responsible for creating a display of art work for our troop. In the display were several paintings of Indian life and model of a canoe.

Although the teachers at school did not encourage us to use Indian language and customs, they did accept my paintings of Indian life. They encouraged my artistic abilities and took a greater interest in me than my previous teachers had taken. I was pleased because the teachers at Pipestone were constantly giving me art projects to do. All these things added to my enjoyment of school and gave me a comfortable feeling of acceptance that had an important influence on my future career.

By the time I entered Red Lake Senior High, my experiences at Pipestone had given me the confidence to get involved in many extracurricular activities. I had always been very interested in music, as well as in art. I was a member of the school choir and band at Pipestone, and I continued these activities in senior high school. The instruments I liked most were the tenor saxophone and clarinet. At Red Lake High, four fellow students and I formed a small dance band with three saxophones, a trumpet, and a drum. We had mostly summer bookings, and we played for the tourists in the areas surrounding Red Lake. We were never sure whether we were popular because of our talent, or because we were an Indian combo —a novelty in those days. But whatever the reason, we enjoyed the experience and the exposure to people from all over the country.

Summer was a time for work, too. During high school I had a summer job with the Civilian Conservation Corps (CCC). This was an agency authorized by the Federal government to hire unemployed young men for jobs in conservation. At Red Lake, we lived in a camp on the reservation. Our job was to maintain and improve the forest environment. We cleaned along the roadways, pulled gooseberry bushes, which are harmful to tree growth, and dug fire breaks. This was hard manual labor, but I liked it until I developed a severe allergy to poison ivy. In the summers that followed, I did building maintenance jobs for the Red Lake Tribal Agency.

# 8 GROWTH OF AN ARTIST

The experiences and opportunities that I had during my three years at Red Lake Senior High School had a strong influence on my choice of a future career. For the first time in my life as a student, I felt free to express myself through art and to do some of the creative things I wanted to do. There were not many students who were involved in art activities, because art courses were not offered then. Most of my art work involved making decorations and scenery for school proms and plays. Although it was usually a lot of hard work, I liked creating scenery for the plays. This experience, no doubt, had a lot to do with my future interest in mural art.

One of my high school teachers remains very dear in

my memories because of her encouragement and her deep personal interest in my art abilities. This kind and compassionate lady was Miss Ross, my English teacher, and she played an important role in my decision about my future. Miss Ross directed all the school plays, so of course I worked under her supervision in creating the sets. Many times, if I had finished my assignments, she let me cut her classes to sketch or work on art projects.

Miss Ross's attitude was different from that of the other teachers, who could not imagine the Indian student in any environment other than the reservation. She often said, "Some day I want to hear great things about you." These words motivated my growing curiosity about art and about career opportunities in other parts of the country. Miss Ross encouraged me to explore the field of art, and she kept me supplied with art materials, art publications, and books that she bought with her own money. Before going home to St. Paul on weekends or vacations, she would ask me what materials I needed. I looked forward to her return, so I could see what materials she had picked out for my work and study.

Miss Ross was interested in Chippewa culture, so I felt free to continue sketching my people and their customs. After my exposure to the white people's way of life, I found that I had a renewed interest in the Indians' life at Red Lake. Many of the Indian customs were becoming more and more meaningful to me, and I continued to observe them and to record them on paper. The colors and the symbolism of Chippewa beadwork designs were among the things I began to research and sketch.

After Christmas vacation in my senior year, I had to decide what career to pursue. My art work was becoming more professional, and I could begin to imagine a career in the commercial art field. So I asked Miss Ross to bring books from the city libraries that would tell me more about commercial art. A career in music also sounded interesting, but I decided that it would require too much travel and expense. As the final weeks of high school passed, I became more certain that art would be a practical way for me to earn my living in the white man's world. My decision became final when I received a year's scholarship to study art at Arizona State College in Phoenix. This award was presented to me at graduation by the Bureau of Indian Affairs. During the following summer I continued to work for the tribal council, doing house painting and maintenance, and saving my money for clothes and the trip to Phoenix.

At Phoenix many new doors were opened for me. I enrolled in art appreciation classes at Phoenix State College. These courses introduced me to the work of the great artists of the world, and I began learning to analyze differences in the styles and designs of various artists. Such courses are common now, but they were completely new and fascinating to me then.

I also found that other Indian students from the Southwest were painting in a completely different style than I was. My style was almost photographically realistic, whereas they presented their subject matter in a flat, profile style that reminded me of ancient Egyptian art.

I lived at the Phoenix Boarding School, which was just a few blocks from the Phoenix Indian School. In the afternoons I took various classes at the Indian school. This is where I learned about mural painting and the preparation of fresco, which is a process of painting on wet plaster walls with water-based paint. My Southwestern friends and I worked as a team, combining our different styles to create an interesting end product. This was a great experience in communication for all of us.

I also took classes in pottery and the preparation of art materials, and these classes added to my knowledge of art. But the more I learned about other forms of art, the more I saw that sketching and painting were the best ways for me to use my talents.

# PART THREE

## TWO ROADS TO follow

Each of Patrick Des Jarlait's experiences seemed to bring him closer to becoming a successful artist. For Patrick, every experience offered a chance to grow and to add to his knowledge about both white and Indian cultures.

After he left school, Patrick served in the military. There he learned some of his most important skills as a commercial artist. After this, his interests began to develop along two separate but parallel paths. He followed one path in order to earn a living with his talents. The other path led him to earn a lasting reputation as a painter of his people.

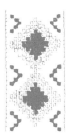

# 9 EXPLORING NEW HORIZONS

Toward spring, when the school term at Phoenix was ending, I realized that I would have to go into military service. This was during World War II, and the Japanese Air Force had just attacked the U.S. naval base at Pearl Harbor. All young men in the United States had to contribute to the war effort.

One day, a teacher from the Indian school called me to his office. There I was greeted by a tall, impressive white man, dressed in a buckskin jacket, boots, and a western hat. He introduced himself as a representative of the Department of Indian Affairs and the United States Army. This gentleman wanted to interview me because of the recommendations of my teachers. He offered me a job as art supervisor in a Japanese relocation camp at Poston, Arizona. Relocation camps were restricted areas where many Japanese-American people were sent by the United States government. After the Pearl Harbor attack, there was strong public opinion in the United States against all Japanese people, including those who had been born in the United States. Because of this, the government relocated, or moved, thousands of Japanese-American citizens out of their homes and into these relocation camps.

Someone was needed at the Arizona camp to organize an art department and to supervise the printing of a camp newspaper. I accepted the position and moved to Poston after the school term ended. Poston was in the middle of the desert, and the climate and temperature there were unbelievable, especially for a young Indian from Red Lake, Minnesota. Temperatures climbed to 135 degrees every day, and it seemed that the wind seldom ceased. The wind blew so much dust into my room that maids had to sweep it three times a day to keep it clean.

Some of the Japanese people at the camp were very talented and had strong art backgrounds. Many of them had worked in Hollywood movie studios before their relocation. These people appreciated having art projects to do, to keep them occupied in their strange new environment. I had great sympathy for the Japanese, because they had been placed in a situation similar to that of my own people. They were forced to move from their homes to remote and restricted areas, as many Indians had been forced to do.

Apparently our art department at the camp was successful, because we got approval to experiment with various kinds of art in addition to working with the printing press. My superiors also gave me permission to take our group of artists into the mountains on Sundays to sketch and paint. We had art shows, too, and these little shows displayed an array of talent in painting, ceramics, watercolor, lithograph, and sculpture. Government employees donated money for the prizes at these shows.

Five months after this department was organized, I received orders for induction into the navy. I reported to San Diego, California, where I was issued a uniform and was scheduled for seamanship training. But after a month of this duty, I was transferred to the Visual Aids Department at the base.

This department produced instructional films and brochures for the navy. The films were used to demonstrate the assembly of torpedos and other such jobs. Many of these films were animated, and they were created by 14 talented animation artists from the Walt Disney and MGM studios. Working with these artists, I learned many skills that prepared me for the future I hoped to have in commercial art.

For the next three and a half years, I worked in the Visual Aids Department and got to know my fellow artists. On weekends we were free to leave the base, and several of the artists rented old garages in the area and fixed them up to use as studios. After the garages were cleaned and painted, they became pleasant places in which to work. During this time, the subjects for my weekend painting came from my memories of Red Lake. Friends who saw my work told their friends about the unusual colors and subject matter, and eventually I was asked to have a one-man show at the Fine Arts Gallery in San Diego. Every painting was sold by the end of the show.

In 1945, shortly after this show, I was discharged from the navy. Without hesitation I was homeward bound.

# 10 THE ARTIST RETURNS TO RED LAKE

It was good to be back at Red Lake. I knew that I would eventually have to look for a job in commercial art, but first, it was important for me to take the time to develop a painting style of my own. I spent the next year experimenting with pencil and tracing paper and doing sketch after sketch. Finally I arrived at a style that satisfied me. The painting of "The Red Lake Fishermen" was the first example of the brush technique and style that became my trademark.

"The Red Lake Fishermen" and all my following paintings were done with watercolors. Bright colors have always been interesting to me, and I used very little water to dilute my pigments. Mixed this way, my paint was thick and kept its vibrant color.

Before working on the actual painting of "The Red Lake Fishermen," I spent many hours observing and sketching the fishermen at work in their boats. Next, I sketched my painting on the final piece of composition material and painted the background areas in with a large brush. Then, with a very small brush, I began to fill in these areas with a series of small brush strokes. These were usually applied to create a rounded, moving effect, and to keep the viewer's eye focused on the points of interest in the painting. I wanted to keep the eye moving within the picture by guiding it with a multitude of tiny brush strokes. These individual little strokes were to me like the tiny little particles that make up our world and everything in it. I worked hard to perfect my technique, and I probably took three times as long as most artists to complete a painting.

The year I spent at Red Lake was a time for keen observation. I wanted to record everything I could learn about my people and their way of life. I had strong personal feelings about keeping my subject matter unique and original, and I also felt compelled to tell the story of my people through my paintings. I have always wanted to show viewers the interest and pride that the Indians take in their families, their ceremonies, and their environment.

After a year at Red Lake, it was time for me to look for

a way to earn a living with my artistic skills. I knew I would someday use the storehouse of information I had gathered for my painting. But I thought that the immediate solution to my need for financial support would probably come from a job in commercial art. In commercial art I could use the background I had gotten in the navy. I began looking for a job in the Twin Cities area of Minneapolis and St. Paul, approximately 300 miles south of Red Lake. The knowledge and skills I had acquired through the years since high school eventually got me a job at Reid Ray Films, Inc., in St. Paul.

During the years that followed, I worked as both a free-lance and a full-time commercial artist. I took jobs at various film companies and advertising agencies and spent a number of years with the visual aids department of Northern Ordnance. One of the highlights of my commercial art career was an assignment from Campbell-Mithun Inc., which is one of the largest advertising companies in the Midwest. Along with some other artists, I was chosen to create a new television advertising campaign for the Theodore Hamms Brewery. We worked for many days over our drawing boards, only to come up with several ideas that were rejected. The company wanted to project a "great out-of-doors" image. Their theme was "Land of the Sky Blue Waters," and it seemed that an animated drawing of some woodland animals might be the answer. One of the most mischievous and delightful animals of the forest is the bear. At Red Lake, the Indians knew that bears were not harmful unless they were aggravated. We usually found them playful, involved in simple pranks like tipping over garbage cans. After I had sketched quite a few animations of the playful woodland bear, I presented the idea to my superiors. They liked my ideas, and so did the Hamms Brewery. The creation of the Hamms bear was one of the most delightful accomplishments I've had in commercial art.

For 26 years I enjoyed a varied career in commercial art. But during those years, I kept turning back to doing what I had always wanted to do—painting my people. I always set aside a few hours each evening after work, and these hours I devoted to personal creation and expression. My lovely wife, Mona, and my five children gave me the courage and the motivation to go on with my painting. Finally, I began to concentrate all my time and energy on painting rather than on commercial art.

I had the good fortune to win recognition and a number of awards throughout the country. Companies, galleries, and private collectors purchased many of my paintings of Chippewa life. Finally, my dreams of what I wished to accomplish had become a reality.

As time went on, my life came to revolve completely around painting and around lecturing at public schools, colleges, and other educational institutions. I always sensed the deep interest that students had in Indian culture. Even the little children listened intently to my lectures on Chippewa customs for long periods of time.

Each of my paintings tells a story about some aspect of Chippewa life. It has always been my hope that my paintings will help to remind my people of their own heritage and that they, in turn, will inform other people about the traditional Chippewa way of life.

Patrick Des Jarlait always worked to preserve the dignity of Chippewa traditions and to promote a better understanding of the American Indian people. Before his untimely death on November 5, 1972, he had built a national reputation as a painter of life at Red Lake. Through his paintings and through his own story of his life, he continues to inspire respect and understanding for the ways of his people.

# BOOKS ABOUT THE FIRST AMERICANS

NON-FICTION

The American Indian in America, Vol. I
*Prehistory to the End of the 18th Century*

The American Indian in America, Vol. II
*Early 19th Century to the Present*

Among the Plains Indians

The Collector's Guide to American Indian Artifacts

Indian Chiefs

Let Me Be a Free Man
*A Documentary History of Indian Resistance*

Patrick Des Jarlait
*The Story of an American Indian Artist*

The Red Man in Art

We Rode the Wind
*Recollections of 19th Century Tribal Life*

FICTION

Prisoner of the Mound Builders

Hunters of the Black Swamp

Claw Foot

We specialize in publishing quality
books. For a complete list please write:

 LERNER PUBLICATIONS COMPANY
241 First Avenue North, Minneapolis, Minnesota 55401